I've Been Called Away

I've Been Called Away

Chester Graham

Introduced by

Geoffrey Lehmann

PUNCHER & WATTMANN

First published in 2023
Published by Puncher & Wattmann
PO Box 279
Waratah NSW 2298

info@puncherandwattmann.com

NATIONAL
LIBRARY
OF AUSTRALIA

A catologue record for this book is available from The National Library of Australia.

ISBN   9781923099029

Cover design by David Musgrave

Printed by Lightning Source International

Chester – the unknown poet

An uncompromising avant-gardist when young, Chester wrote brilliant poetry and strongly influenced younger friends he mentored. The names of some of them – Robert Hughes and Clive James – are familiar to Australian readers. But not Chester. When I googled "Chester Philip Graham", I was startled by the small number of hits – just two items at the top of my screen, and a third lower down. Even nondescript writers tend to have a large internet presence. This personal obscurity may be something he chose.

Chester is the first Australian poet to write poetry in the jokey, colloquial style of what is known as the New York school – poets such as John Ashbery, Frank O'Hara and Kenneth Koch, who threw phrases at the page like an action painting, and treated meanings as objects to toy with and abandon. Ten years younger than the founding members of the New York school, Chester was writing poems like theirs at about the same time – starting in the second half of the 1950s. He is unlikely to have read their work.

How did this bisexual, apolitical, anti-academic young ironist and perfectionist suddenly appear in bourgeois, wholesome Australia? One way of explaining Chester is that he began using words as the avant-garde composers he admired used sound. Chester admired Edgar Varèse – his musical collisions. Like the New York school poets, Chester may also have been stimulated by visual artists. In 1956 the *Direction 1* exhibition in Sydney of non-figurative works by artists such as Robert Klippel and John Olsen provoked what has been described as "a fiercely contested debate" about abstract versus figurative art. But above all, Chester was himself. Only some of his poems employ a baroquely modern complexity. Many have a scalpel-like clarity. Their simplicity can be confronting.

Like Rimbaud, he was a dedicated poet for only a short period – perhaps from the mid-1950s until about 1962. Then he seems to have stopped, apart from some occasional poems later in his life.

In *Unreliable Memoirs* Clive James claims that in his first week of university he read a poem by "Spencer" (who is Chester) in the student newspaper. Clive was so excited, the badges on his jacket rattled. This exciting poem was about Rimbaud's cigar.

The *Honi Soit* for March 4, 1957 – Clive's first week at Sydney University, and mine as well – can be accessed on the internet. On page 7 Chester has a confusing science fiction story – "The Electronic Lavatory" – about a John Pilgrim. An illustration by Robert Hughes shows Pilgrim standing in what seems to be a dunny hole. Four large hands rising out of smaller dunny holes are about to attack him. The heroic Pilgrim's two much smaller hands are also emerging from small dunny holes, and are delicately poised above a typewriter – manual, not electronic. There is no poem about Rimbaud's cigar. But the reference to Rimbaud was spot on. A Rimbaud with his hands delicately poised above a typewriter.

***

When I googled "Chester Philip Graham", the first hit was his death notice:

> Philip Michael (Chester) Graham, poet, playwright, novelist, linguist, translator, interpreter, teacher and actor, born February 6, 1936, died on Monday February 8, 2021, aged 85. He will be missed by his many friends, his lover Michael, and by his ex-wife Barbara and grandson Gabriel who live in Brazil.
>
> A wake will be held at the Lord Wolseley pub, Ultimo on March 15 from 3pm.
>
> RSVP Carlotta …

About 40 of us came to Chester's wake, which was held on the small lawn with trees – a closed-off street – outside the Lord Wolseley in the inner city Sydney suburb of Ultimo. It was a sad and cheerful occasion – a gathering of friends rather than a gloomy assembly of former business associates and family. Many Sydney Realists were there. This is a discussion group – a successor of the Sydney Push – organised by Marion Manton. Chester often came to the Realists' meetings.

He also regularly attended *Players in the Pub*, a play-reading group that began in the suburb of Glebe in 2009. At the wake Lyn Collingwood and Alan Walker from the *Players* read a recent skit by Chester about City Rail – quickly alternating voices telling commuters how to behave and where to go. *Chester was still writing skits!* Lyn and Alan had performed in some of Chester's skits in the 1960s.

His revue skits from the mid-1950s to the early 1960s – many co-authored with Clive James and John Cummings who became Katherine Cummings – were centrepieces of what is known as the Golden Age of Sydney University revue. Chester's recent City Rail skit was genial and mild. His skits from 60 years ago were brutal, brilliant, highbrow farces. "Rasputin; or Ten Days that Dimmed the Lights" (coauthored with Clive James) ends with Rasputin dying on stage from arsenic poisoning, as a fire is starting, a ball is beginning, and the ice-cream is melting upstairs.

At the wake the sociologist Eva Cox was one of the first to speak. When she was a student in the 1950s, she had lived with Chester. They were lovers, she told us, but led strictly separate lives – together, but not together.

Terry McMullen, who has specialised in the history and philosophy of psychology, talked about calling in on Chester and John Cummings in the 1950s. Sharing digs, they were hosting a Sydney University Players rehearsal. Terry listened to these two young polymaths talking, and could hardly believe his ears. He was just a new boy from the country and was astounded by their wild and radical political views. He knew the Labour Party, the Liberal Party, the Country Party and the odd Commo: but Chester and John declared themselves to be Fascists! How were they followers of Mussolini and Sir Oswald Mosely? He realised that there was a new culture to be faced at Sydney University.

A friend from the Greens Party had known Chester towards the end of his life. She spoke about his involvement in Green politics – how supportive he had been. Chester's lover, Michael Aaronson, a softly spoken American perhaps in his sixties, spoke about their life together in recent years, a caring and sharing life.

I read Chester's poem "Cogito Ergo Sit" twice – a poem I know by heart. I explained Chester's Latin title after my first reading. This translates as "I think therefore it should be" – "sit" being the subjunctive third person singular of "esse" – "to be". The title, I suggested, seemed to be one of Chester's jokes. It was a parody of Descartes' famous "Cogito Ergo Sum" – "I think therefore I am". But it also referred to the famous Rodin sculpture of the thinker who is just sitting. That's what thinkers do. I then read "Cogito Ergo Sit" a second time.

Towards the end of the wake I sat down on a seat under the trees next to Katherine Cummings. I had not spoken to Katherine for sixty years – when she was John Cummings, a serious-looking young librarian, dressed in suit and tie who worked in the Fisher Library at Sydney University. Katherine and I had corresponded in recent years. She had sent me her memoir *Katherine's Diary: the story of a transexual.* The cover showed Katherine standing full-frontal in the surf, in a tight white bikini – proudly – shortly after transitioning at age 51. I wanted to discuss Chester's novel, which she was about to publish, and Chester's poems – to be published after the novel.

I don't recall speakers at the wake discussing how Chester became "Chester". The most reliable account is that in the early 1950s a cat known as "Chester" frequented the office of the student newspaper *Honi Soit.* When the *Honi Soit* cat disappeared, Philip Graham took over the name – he became the cat. Younger friends he mentored – such as Robert Hughes and Clive James – all signed their contributions with their own names. Chester hid behind his nom-de-plume. In later years being known simply as "Chester" may have embarrassed him. He became "Chester Graham".

The second hit on my computer screen when I googled Chester's name was "Sydney Push – Wikipedia". It mentioned "Push personalities who emigrated to the United Kingdom included Clive James, Paddy McGuinness, Chester (Philip Graham)…" There was no other mention of Chester. The article described how the Sydney Push, a large, disparate, hard-drinking bohemian group proselytised free love, libertarian detachment and political anarchism from the mid-1950s to the early 1970s. Anne Coombs's *Sex and Anarchy: The life and death of the Sydney Push* (Viking 1996) has a slightly longer mention of Chester. Coombs is discussing the art critic Robert Hughes's connection with friends in the Push:

> Among these friends were Clive James and a young man called Phillip [sic] Graham, who went by the name of Chester. Chester was a keen actor and poet and was much admired by his peers, who expected great things of him. No one seems to have expected too much of Clive James. But in the sort of twist that no longer surprises, Clive James went on to be famous, whereas Chester disappeared into obscurity, last heard of in South America.

***

I was never close to Chester. Robert Hughes, Clive James and Katherine Cummings could have all written a more intimate portrait of him. But Hughes died in 2012, James in 2019, and Cummings in 2022. I had been an admirer of Chester from a distance. At a 2016 Sydney Push reunion I suggested that he publish a book of his poetry. I offered to help in any way I could. I told him how much I admired his poem "Provincial Report", published in *Hermes* (1961) – Sydney University's annual student magazine. In this poem Pontius Pilate asks his emperor:

> Begging Your pardon, by Your leave
> What do I do with this Jew?

It had influenced many poems I wrote. I sent Chester a follow-up email. He promptly replied (3 February 2016):

Geoff -
This is exciting. I'd been dreaming of finding a jazz group to read verse against, as in days gone by. Jazz hasn't gone by, but it has put on a white tie and tails. Alas, the satanic pokies have chased cabaret and music from our pubs.

The poem about Pontius Pilatus appeared in many versions. The most polished version will be in the keeping of Katherine, who has kept copies of a lot of my writing. I've already phoned Katherine to convey my excitement, and my partner and I'll be spending the weekend in her warm company, celebrating one of my birthdays. Pontius is still a hero of mine. He went on to govern, I think, Bythinia.

I returned to an interest in republican and imperial Rome after my living in fascist and revolutionary Portugal, and in tiers-monde and democratizing Brazil …

> Anne Coombs's Sex and Anarchy
+

I was sent a copy of this book while I was overseas, and found it cold and mean. It didn't even try to show the affection, the respect, and the loyalty that united all of us; the core of brainy people, and the beaded fringe such as me. The ethics, toleration, and acceptance I learnt at the Tudor, at the Assembly, at the George [Sydney hotels frequented by the Push] have been my touchstone. Leaning over the balcony of the Upper Circle inside my skull, several dozen of my friends and idols, many of them dead, have been my critical watchers.

I'll see what Katherine has of mine lying around her cultivated chaos.

> It was good talking to you yesterday
+
And very pleasant talking to you, too.

Cheers!

— Chester

In the months that followed our hopes for the imminent publication of Chester's poems evaporated. The main problem was that he had not kept copies of his poems. Those he could get hold of seem to have come from Katherine Cummings (his co-author of skits for Sydney University revues). Katherine continued on as a librarian until her retirement.

On 26 September 2016 Chester sent me an email with no text and a heading "Verse you may be interested in editing". There were 22 poems as attachments. These are 22 of the 40 poems in this book. I did not feel capable of "editing" such a scrupulous stylist as Chester. I immediately contacted publishers I knew. They responded quickly. One of them advised 22 poems were too few. Another advised lack of government grants was hindering publication.

I emailed Chester, telling him about their responses. On 3 October 2016, with a heading "Game over" Chester replied. ("Fisher" is Sydney University's Fisher Library, "Ellis" is Bob Ellis the journalist and playwright, and "Clivey" is Clive James.)

Geoffrey —
I haven't tried Fisher. I took it for granted that looking for anything in Fisher wouldn't be worth the visit.

I've drawn blanks at the State Library.

I was about to visit the National Library. I wouldn't expect to turn up a further eighty poems there, even if they had all of Arna, Hermes, Quadrant, and other stuff on microfiche.

So we had better forget the mirage of a book of Selected. A book of Rejected would be bigger; no one ever liked my stuff much.

I had been planning a further raid on what Katherine has lying around. She doesn't well know what she has; she wasn't sedulously collecting my stuff, and I wouldn't have expected her to. She's a considerable hoarder.

But it is vexing. Since I've been back in Australia, Ellis read out some lines of mine at lunch one day, from a book he was holding. That's one of the poems I can't trace. And Clivey referred extensively to a lyric of mine in an email that he sent to Katherine. That's another. I would have made it the first of any Selection. And made the last poem a similar piece from the fifties, in much maturer mood, when Eva and I were sharing each other's lives.

Scraps of stuff get mixed in memory; half-lines mate up with their better halves. I've never kept a paper copy of any verse.

"Scraps and raps come back to me

In demotic Potawatami

Oh, hungry birds."

Chester's email then mentions Richard Appleton ("Appo") and Lex Banning ("Lex"):

The same goes for two better poets than me, Appo and Lex. I was talking to one of Appo's widows this week. She regretted that so much of Appo's stuff was lost when he 'turned to non-fiction' ...

I work mornings in a homeless shelter. You turned up as joint editor in a Young Australian Poets anthology in our library. I had thought you might care to edit my stuff. I particularly would have needed someone to ruthlessly jettison.

If you're in town much, you might like to suggest a place to have a drink. I'm not an alcoholic any more, and I'd like to have a yarn with you.

I had asked Chester about a poem of his I remembered. Chester's email answered that he didn't have a copy of this poem, or other poems he had written:

Never had a copy of most of them...

One of the 22 poems Chester sent me was a recent poem written through the voice of Katherine's dog, Flora, begging that Katherine would survive a bypass operation. My email to Chester praised it, and Chester's "Game over" email commented, referring to Pip, who is Katherine's daughter:

> It made Katherine laugh. When daughter Pip read it to her after she'd come out of the anaesthetic, she asked for an encore.
> Flora would have been flattered. She was a natural blonde, and aware of the responsibility that goes with that. No longer with us.

The email then discussed a few typos I'd noticed. It concluded:

> Thanks for your interest and consideration.
> Cheers!

Despite Chester's "Game over" email I continued with enquiries about how his poetry might be published. Some friends had a "self-publishing" company. I emailed Chester suggesting I could arrange to have them publish his poems.

He rejected the idea in an email on 26 June 2018:

> Geoffrey —
> I have not felt competent to reply to you, as your last email left me bewildered.
> 1. If no one's desperate to publish me, then it's fitting that I remain unpublished. This suits any unsuccessful author, such as I've been all my life.
> 2. …You've given me the idea, though, that I might arrange a vanity publishing effort myself.
> A few years ago I had a mate of mine's book printed for him, and a Melbourne publishing contact of Katherine's did a fine job. So I might get those Melbourne publishers to print out my verse, a novel, some stories, and my memoirs…
> 3. The reason I'm able to think so constructively is that the

statisticians have given me fifteen months more chance of life. That means that I'm looking forward as far as Spring 2019, but then, I always was optimistic.

4. I'm still flabbergasted that you should find my verse worth listening to. You're wrong, but thank you for that.

Sincerely

– Chester

Chester had prostate cancer. In March 2021, a few weeks after the wake, Katherine and I exchanged emails about her progress with Chester's novel *It's the Culture*. It appeared under her Beaujon Press imprint several months later. She was getting ready to publish Chester's poems. On Sunday, 15 January 2022 Katherine sent this email:

Dear Geoff,

Sorry to have been so silent but I've been sick; currently in the San Op next Wednesday, which I may not survive.

In that case, will you take back Chester's book of poetry, please? Sorry to ask but needs must.

My daughter Pip is my contact… She'll be in touch.

Hope I'll be in contact myself after recovering.

Regards,
Kate

I emailed Katherine back next day, hoping "all goes well, and in case it doesn't" I promised that I'd have Chester's poems published through one of the small poetry publishers.

Katherine died later that week. Pip and I spoke on the phone. Each weekend she was at her father's house. She was yet to locate where Katherine had stored Chester's poems – possibly on her main computer. Pip added – I could hear the emotion in her voice – "I was with Kate when she sent you the email." A few weeks later Kate's main computer died in the La Niña rains.

Michael Aaronson and I met over coffee in the city to discuss
the publication of Chester's poems. We talked about Chester's life
– his 25 years in Brazil, working as an interpreter and translator
for an international accounting firm, experiences which fed into
his novel *It's the Culture* – an Evelyn Waugh type satire about the
chaotic commercial culture of Brazil. Chester, Michael told me,
used to refer to his two former wives, as "my first ex-wife" and "my
second ex-wife". Michael had met and admired the second ex-wife
Barbara. We briefly talked about Chester's grandson Gabriel – who
gave Chester a judo medal he had won, as a keepsake – and his
daughter Aniela, who was murdered.

We began discussing publication plans for Chester's poetry. We
were concerned by the small number of poems – then 24. (By then
I had found two extra poems by Chester in a box of papers in my
attic.) Michael's eyes suddenly lit up. "There may be another poem,"
he said. "The text message Chester sent me that was the start of
our relationship." He spent some time searching on his phone and
showed it to me – preserved in the cloud from several years ago.
He promised to email it to me that evening, so I could decide. That
evening Michael emailed me Chester's text message. I emailed
Michael back: "Chester's message to you is a poem! Beautiful! That
gives us 25 poems!" It is the final poem in this collection.

***

In the later 1950s on mid-mornings in the Sydney University's
Women's Union cafeteria in Manning House, Chester presided over
a table, where students gathered. It was beside some windows and
furthest from the entrance. His table was where conversations were
wittiest, reputations (literary and non-literary) were made and
unmade, and the most attractive female undergraduates wanted to
to be seen drinking coffee. Chester himself did not go to classes,
but his companions did, and they drifted in after morning lectures.
Robert Hughes, Clive James and John Cummings (who was yet
to become Katherine) were among the regulars at this table. Les

Murray and I were never among them. We sat at a different table. However Chester was someone whom Les still mentioned with respect in later years.

The coffee drinkers at Chester's table were contributors to the weekly student newspaper *Honi Soit* and were involved in university theatricals. In February 2021 Katherine emailed Marion Manton (organiser of the Sydney Realists) to describe how some of this happened:

> ... Chester and I met in 1953 (his first year, my second) and wrote sketches for the 1953 revue. We then went on to take over the culture of the revue, substituting surrealist humour and wit for the earlier reliance on sex, scatology and "dirty" words... In his first two or three years Clive used to come out to my place and read my eclectic collection of books so that his style changed from week to week, depending on whether he had been reading e.e.cummings, S.J. Perelman or Victor Hugo...I was the quiet one of the quartet (Chester, Clive, Bobby Hughes and me) but I made my contribution.
>
> (exits R, sobbing quietly into a fine dimity handkerchief).

In her memoir Katherine described Chester as he was in the 1950s. He had a crew cut and walked with a "loose-jointed, slightly stooped lope" as though "progressing by a series of falling movements". He did not change much over the next 60 years — thin and spindly, rather tall. His light ginger crew cut became dusted with silver, and a few lines appeared in his face. He was relatively ageless. As one of his emails reveal, at the age of 80 he was working mornings in a homeless shelter. He could have passed as a trim-looking 60 year old. Chester's friendship with Kate may be the main reason he came back to Australia. She had remained steadfast. She was personally punctilious until the end.

After they met in 1953, Cummings and Chester became the superstars of university revues, co-writing scripts and acting. These revues were staged in first term. *Honi Soit* continued to come out for most of the academic year. *Katherine's Diary* relates how she and Chester "put a lot of energy" into the student newspaper "writing news stories, sub-editing, proof-reading and generally living-in at the *Honi* office." Chester was moving out of the parental home. He sometimes slept on the *Honi Soit* office floor; or late at night he threw gravel at Katherine's window in her parents' house, and slept on Katherine's floor in a sleeping bag.

Katherine was then, of course, John. She did not tell Chester about her transgender feelings. She cross-dressed in the privacy of her parents' house, when no one was there, and photographed herself. That was all she dared to do. Chester's drinking and his ability to keep her secret worried her:

> I had been the recipient of Chester's confession that he had discovered a tendency in himself to homosexuality and it seemed to me that if he could not keep his own secret he might not be able to keep mine. He was, in fact, bisexual...

Katherine was one year older than Chester. That extra year, and her starting university a year before Chester, were a crucial advantage. Although, as she admits, she was "the quiet one", she was Chester's mentor. Her transgender feelings drove her interest in drama and university revues, which Chester then picked up on, but for different motives. Chester's novel *It's the Culture* reads at times like a series of revue skits. His poetry has the economy of cabaret.

Chester's other mentor at Sydney University was the philosopher George Molnar (not the cartoonist who had the same name). George was a gifted artist. He did a delicate charcoal and wash portrait of John Cummings (as she then was). After joining the Sydney Push, George became a keen gambler and professional philosopher and destroyed all his paintings. He died in August 1999, just a few months before Chester came back to Australia from Brazil.

George's partner, Carlotta McIntosh began preparing a festschrift

George Molnar: Politics and Passions of a Sydney Philosopher. She
asked Chester to contribute. Chester wrote about his friendship with
George in the mid-1950s:

Molnar György by Chester Graham December, 2001
George had a book of photographs of the massacres of the Jews.
Although the photographs were blue, and the book in Hungarian,
he made it all immediate for me. He had seen his aunt gunned
down against the cellar wall of their house in Buda. "So you see
Chester. Because."

Buda was all around us. You could stand a spoon up in his
mother's coffee, the typewriter had double accents, Bartók was
on the record player, and I got the dog's name right after a while.

Not always Bartók. Sometimes we got who I liked then,
Varèse. George would be up and down, switching discs of the
Columbia History of Music. A few bars of something different,
and he mightn't have time to come to rest, but crouch standing,
between up and down.

He liked to see Jonjon and me play the fool. I was supposed
to be seventeen at the time, but nobody was taken in. George
had been schooled by Horthy, Hitler, and Stalin. "Because you
see, Chester. So." Totalitarians have to have it all; your sex, your
death, your living. You are to be their product. There are no better
teachers of the value of clowning. Put Octandre on again. Let's
hear it right through this time.

Our attitude paid off at Sydney University. George submitted
his term paper. On utopias, I imagine. Utopias were on our minds
in 1953. The Philosophy academic thanked him, but found it
short weight. Jonjon and I recast it. In what would later become a
rigorous linguistics tradition, we rewrote phrases:

and → Added to this is the fact that

but → It might, however, on the other hand, be argued

if → Should, accordingly, the hypothesis be pertinent that.

This was heady. It went beyond schoolchildren's jokey
translations. It embraced translation:

relevant to the human condition → relevant to the human condition (La Condition Humaine).

There is a verb in Hungarian that means "to take the cabbage out of". We reversed the process, to the glee of George's academic. He praised the term paper, now with added fibre.

When I rented my first room at the Cross, I spent all my money on paperbacks, to fill the width under the window. To show George. No record player, but a radio and cigarettes and booze. "So, Chester. So many books. Mmm. All fiction." Fiction sounded Fixion. He lent me Shirer's The Rise and Fall of the Third Reich. "Can I trust it, George?" "The references, yes. The references are sound."

The Philosophy that he taught may not have been sound; Philosophy is not sound the way that references can be, the way that Bartók is. I would trust it to be light on cabbage, though. Because.

George never actually got to pronounce the word Because. You heard it as Beak Hose. I saw, though. Mmm. So.

What surprised me most, when Carlotta emailed this memoir to me, was that Chester was an early fan of the music of Edgar Varèse, the French-American avant-garde composer — a taste he seems to have acquired from George. The memoir mentions Varèse's *Octandre* for seven wind instruments and double bass, composed in 1923. Thirty years later — in 1953 — Varèse's musical language was still radical. Varèse advocated music as "organised sound", "sound as living matter", "musical space as open rather than bounded", and having "sound-masses" that collide with reverberations. He called for a "crusade for new instruments".

There are two streams in Chester's poetry. One is relatively straightforward: his love of cabaret and concision. The other, adopting the language of Varèse, is experimental: "words as living matter", "statements as open rather than bounded", "phrases colliding with reverberations", or more sententiously, a "crusade for new meanings". Chester's attraction to Varèse explains this second stream. Was Chester also influenced by Ern Malley, the bogus modernist poet concocted by the Australian poets James McAuley and Harold Stewart in 1943? Malley, described by the American poet and critic David Lehman as "the greatest literary hoax of the twentieth century", influenced the New York school of poets.

***

Katherine Cummings and George Molnar were two of Chester's mentors. Chester in turn mentored Robert Hughes and Clive James when they began Arts I at Sydney University in 1956 and 1957 respectively. Hughes was "Bob" to all who knew him. I shall call him that here. He came fifth in the State of New South Wales in the 1955 Leaving Certificate in 1955, and first in English. Then in the following year he flunked Arts I and lost his Commonwealth scholarship. He was following a tradition established by Chester who had done the same in 1953 – failing Arts I and losing his scholarship. But Chester continued this for the next few years – enrolling in Arts I, attending few, if any, lectures and failing until at least 1957.

Bob, like Chester, had been a boarder at St Ignatius College, otherwise known as Riverview – a Jesuit high school for boys from leading Catholic families. The brief biography Katherine wrote for Chester's novel mentions:

> Chester was parked in a Roman Catholic boarding school where he divided his time between winning academic awards and absconding from the school whenever possible.

Chester's last year at Riverview was 1952. Bob's memoir *Things I Didn't Know* has a riveting chapter about what life was like for a young, sensitive boarder at this elite Jesuit high school. It's likely that Chester's years at Riverview were broadly similar. Being three years apart, they would not have known each other. To discourage homosexuality, boys in the senior school couldn't talk to boys in the middle school, and boys in the middle school couldn't talk to boys in the junior school.

Riverview seems to have given Chester and Bob an outstanding literary education. They appeared "brilliant" to fellow undergraduates coming to university from Protestant and government schools. When Bob left Riverview he was able to recite the entirety of some Shakespeare plays and T S Eliot's *The Waste Land* "word-perfect and by heart". *Things I Didn't Know* has several pages explaining the military origin of the Jesuits. When Chester and Bob were boarders at Riverview, the school was still imbued with this militant form of Catholicism. The schoolmaster priests disciplined boys with a leather strap. Each priest was known for his distinctive technique.

Riverview boys were told to fear sex for its own sake – as Vice, "the big enemy". Masturbation caused the leakage of vital fluid from the spine and paralysis past the age of 60. Some boys must have believed this. At Shore, the Anglican school I attended, we cheered the local doctor when he gave the sex lecture and told us masturbation was perfectly harmless.

Bob's memoir describes his schoolboy crises of conscience. Riverview boys losing their faith – as Chester and Bob both did – faced a dilemma. What would they say at Confession? They had to confess, to be free of sin when they took the sacrament – the small wafer – at Mass. They made themselves conspicuous if they did not take the sacrament.

Bob never absconded from high school. Chester's alienation may have been more extreme, with his mixture of "academic awards and absconding". Searching a USB stick with the contents of Chester's computer, I found among various poetic fragments this crude and angry summary of his religious education:

Communion

I believe in one god
That makes it simple
He makes it easy for

Folk like me to follow

He likes me to follow folk
Who know me to be simple
They and I have one god
Who is easy to swallow.

The outstanding literary education Riverview gave Chester and Bob was in some ways a minus for them. Arts I may have appeared "too easy", almost boring. Riverview's regimented culture also had a darker side. Their escape left them directionless when they started at university. Chester eventually obtained a degree – many years later in Linguistics at Reading University in England. Bob's loss of direction was temporary. He enrolled in Architecture in 1957 – his studies financed by his older brothers.

I witnessed a strange event when I started Arts I in 1957. Chester came to one of the first English lectures for the year, entering through a side door, down at the front of the raked lecture hall – the Wallace Theatre. This held about 300 students. He was accompanied by two attractive girls, one dark-haired, the other fair, and perhaps a young man. I was aware that Chester was enrolled for this course. The members of his entourage did not seem to be English I students. They may have been there as witnesses of Chester's sitting through the lecture.

In an email to me many years later Clive wrote: "What I love most about my memory of the English I lectures was the bare-facedness with which Prof Mitchell recited a chapter of his little book every week, verbatim." The lecture Chester attended may have been one of Prof Mitchell's verbatim recitals. Chester and his entourage sat attentively through it, as though it was a ceremonious Dada event. (Chester did not always require an audience for his Dada performances. Katherine once found him tearing pages out of a book as he finished reading them.)

When Clive James started Arts I in 1957, Katherine Cummings's "quartet" was now complete. Bob's *Things I Didn't Know* refers to this quartet as "a groupuscule of wits whose mannerisms had to be imitated".

Here is how Clive introduces Chester in his *Unreliable Memoirs* (1980). He is describing the temporary *Honi Soit* stand called the Flying Saucer, which was set up in Science Road during his first week of university (Orientation Week):

> ...it was crammed with these exotic creatures, the like of which I had never seen... I had turned up in my school blazer, but in order to indicate that I was a man of parts I had pinned my Presbyterian Fellowship badge to the lapel, alongside the Boys' Brigade badge in my buttonhole...

Clive's rough brio (despite his Christian indicia) seems to have immediately attracted Chester, as he later attracted many women. Chester welcomes Clive with a line of passive aggressive patter:

> "My God... it's a Christian! Come and work for *honi soit*. We need a broad spectrum of opinion. You could offset the influence of Wanda here. She's a witch...

Chester signs Clive up to join the *Honi Soit* staff next day, then makes oxymoronic remarks about his jacket:

> "Those badges are distorting the shape of what could be a perfectly good jacket, if it were a different colour and cut."

Chester hands Clive a copy of *Honi Soit*. Clive finds a poem by Chester in it — about Rimbaud's cigar. Although the existence of such a poem is "unreliable", Clive describes more reliably his reaction:

> The vividness of the language was extraordinary. Even when crammed into symmetrical verse forms every sentence sounded like speech. I can't say that my future course was set there and

then, but neither can I say that it wasn't. I was so excited that my badges rattled. There were sparks coming off my lapel.

Next day in the *Honi Soit* office Clive listens to chitchat between "Spencer" (who is Chester) and "Keith Cameron" (John Cummings):

> As they worked, Cameron and Spencer kept up an exchange of allusive wit that I found at once daunting and exhilarating. Spencer called something Firbankian. Who, what or where was Firbankian? I was lost, yet not in the usual way of feeling that I ought to be somewhere else. Somehow I knew that I was in exactly the right spot.

Unreliable Memoirs describes (again unreliably) the first University Revue Clive attended. Spencer and Cameron were in charge, and wrote all the scripts. "The décor by Huggins" (Robert Hughes) was "brilliant" – when you could actually see it. Spencer's love of ultraviolet lighting and mist from dry ice didn't add to its visibility. There were two sketches about Virginia Woolf and a third may have been about Gertrude Stein. A willowy girl wearing a gown of shaving mirrors seemed disappointed that a torch song had not been written for her, and instead had to read a poem by John Crowe Ransom while "Spencer stood on one leg in the background, softly tapping a gong." (The reading of a poem by Ransom, the elegant, academic formalist from Tennessee, is truly bizarre – e. e. cummings yes, but Ransom?)

Unreliable Memoirs summarises (more reliably) Clive's first exposure to high culture:

> I suppose that first year of university was just about the most ridiculous phase of my life. It was love again, of course, but this time I was in love with all of them. I copied Spencer's walk, talk and gestures. I copied the way he wrote. I copied the way Keith Cameron read...

Cameron's way of reading directed Clive back to a more traditional mainstream. As a lifelong fan of traditional jazz, Clive seems never to have shared Chester's interest in avant-garde composers such as Varèse. Or the avant-garde in general. He became uncomfortable with some aspects of Chester:

> Spencer lost in the toils of a fully bisexual love life and a chronic deficiency of funds, hardly ever read anything except science fiction. I soon realised that his *pronunciamentos* on literature in general were based on the most evanescent acquaintance with its individual products. But Cameron... had an impressive private library of modern literature. I devoured it author by author... Cameron was less capricious. His level head was the necessary corrective for Spencer's influence.

It seems most of all, Clive was comfortable with Huggins. Huggins smoked cigarettes "two feet long" and "had a face so handsome it was like a cartoon, his hair blond and abundant". Clive admired "his grace, ease, creative fertility and ... beautiful girlfriends". Clive was the youngest member of the quartet. It may have been "ridiculous", but 1957 was his damascene year. His combination of serious literary ability and showmanship is unusual. This basic formula came from Chester. Clive took it and transmuted it in places none of his friends would have believed was possible.

In September 1960 two university drama groups jointly performed George Bernard Shaw's *Heartbreak House*. Chester reviewed the performance in *Honi Soit*. He wrote of his future "first ex-wife":

> Lady Utterword, gave us the best female performance of the evening. Miss Sue Taylor looked wonderful and has an exciting voice, with more range than her acting, which was admirable. We see a lot of Lady Utterword in this play, and I never tired of her.

Susan Taylor – a classic blonde with an American accent – and Chester began seeing each other after this review. They were later married in the grand salone in the Campidoglio by the mayor of Rome, whom Susan describes as "a tubby little man in a tricolore sash that covered him like a bedspread". The witnesses were Bill Pinwill (the dashing, dark-haired Australian journalist) and his future wife, Sally. The officials could not comprehend Bill's surname. It had to be spelled out as "Pisa Imola Napoli Vashington Imola Livorno Livorno" – a concatenation of city names like a line of dialogue from a Chester skit. Chester's surname was "Genova Roma Ancona hotel Ancona Milano".

Chester and Susan lived together in London in a brief marriage. They included Sydney University revue items in a show, *Guarding the Change* (1965), which they staged at the Lyric Theatre Hammersmith. Susan Taylor is now Susi Papi, and lives with her husband outside Rome. She commented on an earlier version of this preface:

> Chester had more or less stopped writing poetry by the time we met, or, at least, it never occurred to him to show me any. I never did understand what it was that attracted him to me (apart from the obvious). What attracted me to him was the same thing everyone else was dazzled by, that extraordinary brain unencumbered by self esteem. I don't think he ever thought particularly highly of my brain.
>
> I very much like your observation that Clive was neither shy nor uninterested in fame, which is neatly understated. In London in 1963-4, during a period in which he spent more time at our cold water walk down than anywhere else, I grew tired of being treated as a sort of superior domestic servant whose principal purpose was to go to work to earn enough to support all three of us. I remember one party at which someone must have offended his particularly touchy amour propre and he stormed off into the night screaming in the middle of the street that he was going to be famous and when he was he would never speak to any of us again. I was quite pleased about that.

After obtaining his degree in Linguistics from Reading University Chester moved to Portugal. The only manuscript of his first novel was lost to an incoming tide on a beach near Oporto. One chapter of *The Pikers*, survives – Chapter 18, "The Mother of the Deceased", published in *Hermes* (1960). After Portugal's Carnation Revolution of 1974 Chester moved to Brazil. When the Brazilian economy collapsed, he sold his house in Brazil to pay his taxes and came back to Australia on the last day of 1999.

***

By 1875 all of Arthur Rimbaud's poems were written; he had given up on poetry and began his travels. He was just 21. In 1880 he settled in Aden, then a few years later in Ethiopia as a businessman, a pioneer exporter of coffee from Harar.

When Chester left Australia, disappearing "into obscurity, last heard of in South America", like Rimbaud he seems to have given up on poetry. Susi Papi's email broadly confirms this. In later life he seems to have had only a vestigial interest in poetry. Chester's partner Michael suggested *I've Been Called Away* as the title for this book. It was something Chester liked to say – "I've been called away". It could be the start of a song. Chester's characteristic poetic mode was cabaret.

None of the poems in *I've Been Called Away* are set in Brazil. The first 31 of the 40 poems in this book seem to have been written about 60 years ago. When Chester sent me his 22 poems, they came as 22 separate attachments. My impression was that the first 14 attachments were all written in Australia before he travelled to Europe – from the mid-1950s until about 1962. They were not in chronological order. "Provincial Report", published in 1961 came before "Park Ward Rolls Royce", published in 1957. As further poems from that period of his life came to light, I inserted them where they fitted comfortably among the 14 poems, without disturbing the order (or disorder) Chester chose for them.

The final 8 attachments he sent – starting with "At St Stephens"

– had a more relaxed tone and more current references. I later found these 8 poems in a computer file he had labelled "21st century", which confirmed they were written after his return to Australia.

When Pip told me Katherine's main computer had died, I began searching Sydney University student publications, starting in 1953. A villanelle "Krishna Wept" written by Alexander Samataplan, a non-existent surname in Google was the earliest possible Chester poem I found. It was published in *Honi Soit*, September 30, 1954. Chester was aged 18 and on the staff of *Honi Soit* at the time. If it is his, it is neophyte Chester – for biographers, not readers. In my hunt for Chester poems I found two notices in the "Frankly You're Too Apathetic" section of *Honi Soit* for May 17, 1956:

> LOST Six tapering wooden cylindrical bodies, one wooden platter with inset metal, and one loosely woven piece of green cloth. NOTIFY LA1855

This was followed by a short advert for the sale of a 1930 Oldsmobile sedan, and below this there was a second notice:

> FOUND Six pieces of wood like blackboard pointers, one cultured vulture on a tray, and one green hair net as used by gentleman. Apply LA 2216

The two notices – I am certain – are a concocted *poème trouvé* by Chester (perhaps with help from Katherine). The ingenuity of their language points to Chester. His poem "Here, my girl" mentions a *green* Morocco wireless set; and the notices refer to a gentleman's *green* hair net. If an actual "gentleman" is being lampooned, he would not have appreciated the implication that he was a "culture vulture". The blackboard pointers indicate he may have been into S & M. Who are the owners of the telephone numbers? LA indicates they were in the vicinity of Newtown, perhaps the university itself!

Chester's poems "The Park Ward Rolls Royce" and "Daylong Byways" were published in Sydney University's *Hermes* (1957) when

he was just 21. Mature and sophisticated in their use of language –
neither of them is the work of a neophyte. "The Park Ward Rolls
Royce" caused a minor sensation among Chester's friends. It was
seen as marking the emergence of a new and important poet –
someone who did more than just write brilliant revue scripts.

"Daylong Byways" is more obscure and perhaps more
interesting. Although Chester was sceptical of his friend George
Molnar's philosophising, he acknowledged the reality of physics,
electronic circuits and the cycle of order and disorder continuing
after human consciousness stops: "This sober current singing".
Along with random experiments with language, he enjoyed
technical precision. "Latterday saints" refers to "sixty cycle light",
and "Autobus, My Autobus" refers to "the fifty cycle hum".
Alternating current frequency is the number of cycles per second,
which can be either 50 or 60 cycles per second.

There were two issues of *Hermes* in 1958. Chester's poem
"Weather Report" appeared in the first issue. It was not among
the 22 poems he sent me. Its casual title is intended to mislead. It
has something of the feeling of the New York school of poets such
as John Ashbery and Frank O'Hara. Take the magisterial opening
verse, for example:

> Birds like aeroplanes stultify
> Those stupefying pigeon rows
> Where beneath the mending shows
> Going up like gentle fireworks
> To heaven, as the Christian Good
> Abide with him who mapped out Hell
> Wrote "Here be lions", was mauled and fell
> To earth in Palestine.

I am not sure what all of this means. Its hinted-at meanings are
untrustworthy promises. But the voice is strangely convincing. The
second verse shares a similar magisterial sound world. It has four
puzzling lines which can be decoded:

> The only show that's worth the tax
> Is watching seedlings grow perhaps
> And fair maidens, all in a row
> Before the flight, the lions and falling.

In the 1950s Australia had an entertainment tax, now completely forgotten, and equally bizarre taxes on gold and flour. Seedlings grow in a row, and Chester is likening the young maidens to seedlings. These are the beautiful girls who enjoyed being seen drinking coffee at his table in Manning House. This is a show that's worth the tax! But there will be a flight, a falling and lions that can maul us. The dedicatee of this poem is "Jenny" — who may be Jenny Towndrow — one of those girls.

Like a change in key, the third verse shifts to a tripping metre of short lines with two or three stressed syllables. It describes this falling of the maidens in its frivolous, light-hearted metre.

> Wheels like doves
> Flying psalms
> Sing inside of her
> Peel like skins
> Of mandarins

The peeling skins of mandarins couplet suggests the loss of the hymen.

On a second or third reading we begin to realise this poem is like a musical theme and variations — slow variations mixed in with quick variations. There are six eight-line stanzas, broken up by two quicker interludes: the first of 14 lines, and the second of 12 lines.

In the later half of the poem the maidens of the early verses are replaced by the dying homosexual and "drowned old lady's smile". There is a reference to T S Eliot's famous phrase "a nation of lost golf balls" — but Chester makes fun of it. It becomes one golf ball. "Weather Report" is about individuals, not nations, and —

Knowing they lose is for the few
And you can not know what hill behind.

You have lost your golf ball, and in a similar way your syntax lost has been. But many of us are unaware of losing anything. Losing is "for the few". The old lady is one of these losers:

Some of these days
She's losing losing
Love all only
Won the toss

A tennis term − "Love all"− is quickly followed by a cricketing term − "Won the toss". The old lady has chosen "love all" and she's losing.

"Weather Report" distracts the reader with wonderful excursions such as:

Weep like others' stars
Irrelevant as motor cars
Falling over Palestine.

Despite its elusiveness and apparent lack of rationality, "Weather Report" may have a meaning. It seems to be a "seven ages of man" poem − or perhaps seven ages of woman. Words such as "loss", "losing" recur. The poem is about loss which may be as irrelevant as "motor cars/ Falling over Palestine" − there is nothing you can do about it. But "love" also recurs as a counterpoint. The two themes join together in the ravishing last line: "Love at least a lost away".

Although Chester was a decade younger than O'Hara and Ashbery, this poem is exactly contemporaneous with poems they were writing that have a not dissimilar feeling. His was an entirely original modernist voice. He can be seen as foreshadowing "language poetry" of the 1970s − language as "a flow of contexts", to quote Lyn Hejinian.

Clive James was being disarmingly accurate, when he wrote in *Unreliable Memoirs*: "I copied the way he wrote." His poem in the very next issue of *Hermes* (issue number 2 for 1958) was directly modelled on Chester poems such as "Weather Report". "A Sadness of Night" begins:

> Cross your heart and hope to die
> She seemed to say there, threaded through
> A chair, a jagged outline in the smoke:
> Feet and glass and gramophone
> Combined to beat in timeless time
> From here on in you're on your own
> —A challenge, painted thinly as a joke.

"A Sadness of Night" sounds like Chester, but lines such as "A chair, a jagged outline in the smoke" are derivative braggadocio – typical of apprentice poets, who love words such as "jagged". Clive soon realised this type of poem was not what he wanted to write, and in a few years became one of the finest Australian poets, but very different from Chester.

Reviewing *Hermes* (No. 1 of 1958) in *Honi Soit*, "E.L." was puzzled by Chester's "Weather Report":

> Chester's poem "Weather Report" has such obvious personal significance that it is difficult to criticise it with any degree of understanding or intelligence. Although it is probably not given to ordinary mortals to understand or even find a theme in the poem, many will be fascinated or at least made uncomfortable by the kaleidoscopic procession of thoughts and images which make it up.

Delusion

It is a common delusion that such a series of apparently disconnected ideas is all that is necessary to make up "modern" verse. This, of course, is not true, and the work of practically any twentieth-century poet affords much more pronounced examples of this "fleeting thought" technique without being as oblique as Chester's poem.

Chester could write with brilliant clarity, as well as elusive emotionality. "I Don't Care" and "Cogito Ergo Sit" were published in *Honi Soit* on 31 July 1962. Both poems are among the 22 poems he sent me. They are about his break with Catholicism.

"I Don't Care" begins:

> I don't care that it rains and freezes
> I am safe with my strange diseases

It is a poem of affirmation. Whatever happens to the poet now, he is indifferent; he can deal with it. The priests threatened him with paralysis past the age of 60 if he allowed his vital spinal fluid to be wasted. But he feels safe with his strange diseases. Now he knows "their god is lying". He is happy rowing "negligent to the cataract". There is even a chance of renewal, dawn coming up "like an artifact". The phoenix which is reborn in flames may crow again.

"Cogito Ergo Sit" is more regretful. I have already explained the meaning of the title and the poem's joking reference to Rodin's statue. Catholicism promised certainty. Chester would like to get it back, but he can't. Instead we have "a million laws of motion" – the great scientific discoveries about space and time in the 20th century. But they don't give us certainty – in fact the opposite is true. We have lost

> The universe that ceased to be
> On Bishop Berkeley's death.

Bishop Berkeley died in 1753. The Internet Encyclopedia of Philosophy explains:

In the Introduction to the *Principles of Human Knowledge*, Berkeley laments the doubt and uncertainty found in philosophical discussions.

I found the classic "The United Kingdom of Great Britain and Northern Ireland" in *Honi Soit* September 11 1962 – a wry satire about convicts being exported from the UK to Australia, and their descendants coming back to the UK and "inspecting their inheritance". You may wonder why beefeaters have "free teeth"? Their teeth are "free" courtesy the UK's National Health Service.

This poem is the last on a two page spread of poems by six other Sydney University poets, including Les Murray. The first poem on the double-spread is "Mary, call the cattle home" by "Anon". It is obviously Chester's. It employs the same ABBA rhyme scheme as his United Kingdom poem. "Mary, call the cattle home" is a parody of Charles Kingsley's "The Sands of Dee". Mary drowns in the Kingsley poem. Before coming home to tea in Chester's parody, she genuflects at the neatly designed shrine for St Gorboduc. Gorboduc was an uncanonised, legendary king of Britain and gave his name to the first English blank verse play The Tragedie of Gorboduc. Like Chester, John Ashbery seems to have been intrigued by the name, and published a poem "Gorboduc" in his volume *April Galleons* (1987).

"The Man Who Killed the Harbour Bridge" is one of the three poems in this book retrieved from Chester's computer. Major Francis de Groot was known as "the man who stole the Harbour Bridge" and has been described as "a fascist sex symbol". At the opening ceremony for the Harbour Bridge in 1932, de Groot rode up on horseback and slashed the ribbon with his sword, just as the socialist State Premier – Jack Lang – was about to cut it. Chester's parody of this event, contains two lines from the hymn "Lead Kindly Light" (written by Cardinal Newman while he was an Anglican clergyman). Chester indented them. As well as indenting them here, these two lines are now in italics.

Like all good poets, Chester has a distinctive voice. The language of a poem such as "Now that I have dared" is so plain, it could be mistaken for prose, apart from the line breaks. We cannot imagine anyone singing "Now that I have dared". But his predilection for cabaret (as his characteristic mode) also keeps Chester's language plain. Many of Chester's poems can be sung – even some densely philosophical poems, such as "Cogito Ergo Sit". You can imagine Marlene Dietrich singing lines such as "Certain is a word I like", "Idle notions, wasted breath", "You cannot bring it back to me …" Chester startles the reader by incongruously mixing philosophy and cabaret – a serious poem presented as a joke.

Chester does not avoid conventional poetic modes entirely. "Bad Lad Ballad" is an example with verses such as:

> My love had honey to soothe my thirst
> Our love was strong as a windlass chain
> Her hair was black as the deepest well
> Her fainting tears as soft as rain.

But the reader quickly realises Chester has employed traditional language to mock it. As well as having a girlfriend in the woods, the poet has a boyfriend on the hill, and has the best of both, until his two lovers meet by accident. The poet exclaims (in the style of a Scots border ballad):

> Curse the day of that fateful chance
> And curse all lovers' deceiving charms
> My love lay where the ferns are thick
> With my love in his arms.

Lesser poets would have ended the poem there – a dramatic high point. But Chester is not just writing a poem, he is coming to terms with his own bisexuality. He concludes:

> Sing a lament for the loss of love
> For my lonely state and my aching heart.
> Now I must seek along my way

A wood and a hill that are far apart.

His last verse is an anticlimax, mocking himself as an Ancient Mariner of bisexuality who should be more careful in the future. This may be the best poem in the English language about the dilemma of bisexuality — perhaps the only one.

Chester was reticent and self-conscious. He wrote about his self-consciousness in "With you here beside me":

> With you here beside me
> Everything is fine
> I can peek, and prove
> Your eyes are watching mine

I found this poem in a box of papers in my attic. It was published in a stapled roneo-ed publication, *Pinchgut Papers* — purple ink on semigloss foolscap. The cover page stated it was "PROVISIONAL ISSUE NO. 2. NOT FOR SALE OR DISTRIBUTION".This non-issue of *Pinchgut Papers* also contained another Chester poem "When Adam delved". Neither was among the 22 poems he sent me.

"With you here beside me" seems to be addressed to a woman. It is an unconventional take on the traditional "Gather ye rosebuds while ye may" theme. Unromantically, the poet is checking that his lover is watching his eyes and decides that he's just one of "A hit parade of stand-ins".

Clive wrote: "I copied Spencer's walk, talk and gestures. I copied the way he wrote". He did not copy Chester's hyper-self-consciousness. If he had, Clive would not have become the suave TV host of later years, whose only parallel may be the Austro-Romanian novelist Gregor von Rezzori, who, as well as writing some of the greatest novels of the 20th century, was the genial, suntanned, aristocratic host of the Austrian TV show *Jolly Joker*, interviewing the rich and famous. "With you here beside me" is uncomfortably honest. Its companion poem "When Adam delved" is more likeable, with its wonderful last verse:

Two knew loneliness
By the lake:
He called it, God;
Eve called it Snake.

I have introduced a dash at the end of the line

Even that we share –

My "editing" of Chester's poems is restricted to this one instance, the use of italics in "The Man Who Killed the Harbour Bridge" and the removal of obvious typos.

The first poem in this book is "Ferry Ride without the Newspaper". If you are expecting an imagistic tour of Sydney Harbour with splashes of yellow sun, blue sky, green water and seagulls, you will be disappointed. The poem is more interested in the physics of motion – "Plug-ugly knockabout lurches out of home" – than in decorative word painting. There is a puzzling passage midway through the poem. The ferry is coming to a stop at a wharf:

Dig heels in the water to stop at the wharf
Eases into it, on the boil, gently
A middle-aged matron kneeling to communion
There's a soft loving shock
To the buoyant jetty, shocking softly the matron
Waiting on it in chilled warmth
If she lives to be a hundred
She'll forget it till her dying day.

I was not worried by the boiling water – from the twin propellors reversing fiercely to halt the ferry – but who was this matron? Was she someone waiting on the wharf? Then I remembered that several ferries in service in the 1950s and 60s were named after women – *The Lady Denman, The Lady Edeline, The Lady Ferguson* and *The Lady Scott* (who had a sex change and became *John Cadman*). Traditionally boats are "she". The matron in the poem is the ferry. She is waiting in chilled warmth, as her diesel engine is water-cooled and running in neutral. Some of these ferries lasted almost a century. So she could live to be a hundred. But she'll forget this moment till her dying day, because she's just a ferry! "Ferry Ride without the Newspaper" is an expressionist tour-de-force.

The poem which follows it – "Albino Girl Bathing" – is imagistic, beautiful and tender – a small miracle. It seems the albino girl is bathing at sunrise, when the sun will damage her least. She is being helped by three laughing friends, who lead her from the water as:

> The sun spreads yellow on the brown reef,
> The tan sand, the blue tide, my darkening hands.

All of these things have colour, unlike the albino girl.

"Hymn" and "Heroics" were not among the 22 poems Chester sent to me, and were a lucky find, discovered by Pip Cummings in Katherine's copy of *Arna* (1958) – which Katherine edited. Robert Hughes provided six illustrations for "Hymn" and "Heroics" when they were published in *Arna*.

There is a sharp dividing line between what poets publish and what they don't. Good poets write some bad poems. That's how they learn their craft. Poems which the poet thought were not good enough to publish, should be left on the unpublished side of the dividing line.

I treated all of of the 22 poems Chester sent to me as "published". I have also included here all his poems that were in student publications and the non-publication *Pinchgut Papers*. Unpublished poems on poets' computers after their death present a dilemma. Michael sent me a USB stick with all Chester's computer files. I found just a few files containing poems. About 20 poems were unfamiliar. Some were scanned from documents hand-written 60 odd years ago. Some were trivia or re-workings of published poems. Three poems – "Love Play", "Pussy's very fond of cream" and "The Man Who Killed the

Harbour Bridge" – had enough memorable lines, that they had to come across from the unpublished side of the line.

I found "Latterday saints", "Here, my girl", "Night is a sleepy Mexican at dawn" and "Pigeons on the grass, by crikey" in 1957 issues of *Honi Soit*. In "Here, my girl", "petty death" refers to "la petite mort" or small death, meaning orgasm. "Pigeons on the grass, by crikey" is about Sydney's Anzac Memorial in Hyde Park. Approached along a long pool of remembrance, a massive structure of pale pink granite houses a central statue on a high plinth, described in the poem. A naked man of black bronze is lying as though on a rack, across a metal shield, with his arms stretched out in a cross. The "dying black men" who stare at him in the poem are "black" perhaps because their suits are dark or have absorbed blackness, the colour of death, from the statue. After exiting ("defiling") from this house of death, the poet (the son of a senior Royal Australian Air Force officer) can cheer himself up, watching a pigeon, bobbing up and down, with its "hinging head". "Black" appears again in the final line of "Autobus, My Autobus" (from a 1962 *Honi Soit*) – "The black conductors come". Here "black" refers to the dark uniforms of the bus conductors as they arrive at the bus depot at 4 am in the morning. This is a wonderfully atmospheric poem about working lives, worthy of William Carlos Williams.

I found "When You Walked" published directly above "Evening Below" on the same page of *Hermes* (1960). I have preserved this pairing. "When you walked" is probably about a woman. She lights up the "burning men", and is "Up for sale/ Evergreen". "Hell, you must have seen" can be read as an imprecation followed by "you must have seen", or read literally.

"When You Walked" is dangerously alive. The people walking in "Evening Below" are strangely nondescript. I was puzzled and vaguely repelled when I first read this poem. I read it several times and looked for clues, as I was writing this preface. The pairing of "Evening Below" with "When You Walked" in *Hermes* (1960) may be significant, or an accident. A more direct clue is a comment in Chester's email of 3 February 2016:

> Leaning over the balcony of the Upper Circle inside my skull, several dozen of my friends and idols, many of them dead, have been my critical watchers.

An email from Chester to Carlotta McIntosh on 29 September 2019, discussing her late partner George Molnar, has a similar comment:

> I'm anti-intellectual, anti-academic. I accept rational thought, if the handle is well-designed and nonstick … George is one of those leaning over the upper stalls inside my brain case, adjudicating my keeping of the decency I learnt from the Push.

The "you" in "Evening Below" is dead, and is looking down on the overcoats gravely walking in the evening below. With its utterly bare language, it may be the most extraordinary poem in this book. "Do you like it now?" Chester keeps asking the dead you.

His cleansed and precise diction does not seem to have changed much from earlier to later poems. But tone and emotion do change. The radical hyper-aesthete of the mid-1950s and early 1960s mellowed. He became more comfortable in his mind and perhaps his ambivalent sexuality. In England he worked as a switchboard operator for British Telecom, helping people to connect, and was finally able to complete a university degree. Later he worked as an interpreter, again helping people to connect, and then in old age in a homeless shelter as a pensioner helping worse-off pensioners. But he did not become extroverted, like Clive or the Jolly Joker, Gregor von Rezzori. He was still reticent. The same quality of language is there in the later poems, occasional as they are. But with less angst. He was not restlessly fertile as Clive continued to be until the end. Chester no longer needed to write poetry.

As he once tore pages out of a book after reading them, he did not bother to preserve his poems, as almost all poets do. Of the 80 or more poems he may have written, at present we have only 40. They are rare and valuable and we should read them slowly and with care.

Geoffrey Lehmann
Lindfield, 2022

Ferry Ride without the Newspaper

Sky then sea
Telescope and snorkel
Seesaws up roll inside out
Volume down to the water cloud
No signature has signed.

It's our ferry that'll start the show
Sky will telescope, you'll see, sooner
Faster than the sea.

The diesel ineptly detaches, grabs
At the air and gets it down
More power to the water as the sparks fly upward
Plug-ugly knockabout lurches out of home
Shoots through the telescope as the waves
Come out as stars for ferries to ride to
Bent paper rocket ship happily propelled
By some clumsy summer thunderstorm deep at work easy
In the sea's streets.

Scenery contracts and whispers in the dark
Stalling forward to beyond the screen
Of shattered skies and clouds of water.

The sights behind are forgotten tissue torn
By the rape of moving. Kill a thing and wonder.
To the sides the poster stretches and breaks
Dissolves, is lost, resolves again
Mutes rappings three sheets in the wind
Flapping like a daily from before the Flood
Snapping ends snarled in the revolving screw.

May this world not come undone
Save piece by piece, in order.

Under the bent wheel of the soggy star
Is the next wharf to call at
When we arrive there
That much is certain.

We fight our own going forward
Dig heels in the water to stop at the wharf
Eases into it, on the boil, gently
A middle-aged matron kneeling to communion
There's a soft loving shock
To the buoyant jetty, shocking softly the matron
Waiting on it in chilled warmth
If she lives to be a hundred
She'll forget it till her dying day.

Stalk into the craft
Clutch the stairs
Preen on the seat
Start again, thank you, take up the bundle
Now we're in the rumble
Seat.

But the sky has tilted
Spills electric raisins
Bouncing up to its rim again
Losing momentum they settle on the surface
We scatter them.

Telescope, sky
Click out some more yet, so much left
In the bottom of the barrel, from gulls to jellyfish
Jellyfish and gulls

Ask each other how they do it.
Their fat day is a left-over mardi gras
From the Hall of Mirrors, going stale.

In relief, the rocks
Shattered across
Wear where they've chewed at the years
Man's faithful friend who eats his heels.
Bones and scraps are the blocks of flats
Stacked back across their backs.
The nested matron peeks with greed
At the stately flats. To live on those bones
But her boat will not stop.

Gulls fly straight in a scorching spiral
Ignoring the unwritten line we follow
Knowing their form as any casting
Loves the shape it's made in.
They counterpoint the moving ferry
Wind of hot metal climbing sideways
Oil as sour as eardrums bleeding
The crocodile tears of a warm guitar.

Here outside the air is cold as salt
Volumes of it meet you, then move away
Draughts in a tube that has no sides
Hollow as toothache, cold as a star
Cold as the bridge that laces the sky
Begins at both ends to get to the middle
So pleased with itself, with its gloating red eye
You know you could kill it, burn out its soul
With a brand of iced flesh.

Shiver the matron
The afternoon is on the turn, will curdle

Now as we tip the wharf, go sour
Now. Now passengers
Claw down from their nests
Walk the plank to drown on land
Bleating, fording the stiles.

Albino Girl Bathing

The sunrise finds her light red eye
Her pale straw hat should hide.

She brings no colours to the sea
That fills her blouse with green.

Her white stocking kicks a rising wave
That lightens and runs back.

Her laughing friends who pull each sleeve
Dip three faces down and up.

She splutters. Empty dazzle stars
The space between the sky and her.

From her silver eyebrows streams
The water that they lead her from.

The sun spreads yellow on the brown reef,
The tan sand, the blue tide, my darkening hands.

Hymn

Plainclothes tiger sitting still
And fitful still, in singing burr
Of hills and harps, old holiness
So slowly unremitting
This intermittent rhythm of bass joy
For cupboard love in idleness.

It could be scarcely hot remorse
For all your race's laziness
In making us your zodiac,
Who run your lives as business managers
Who lurch about and break the Chippendale
And yet who made it.

Sing and die, and dying sing
Of slippered fires and zippered naps
With smoky cosiness repel
The murdering, plundering dog
Who would destroy
And therefore must
And must regret it
As much as you.

Sing to die, but don't reveal
To us who make and break the points
On which you balance to relax
Who you were and what; from where
You come on muffled feet
Rowing with velvet oars through the night's river
To whine of cupboard loveliness
And hot jew's harps of idleness, relax

And be content with legacies
Leavings for your laziness:
Butter and milk and a plate of fish
And a broken, leaking mouse.

Heroics

I. The Proving of Parsifal

PARSIFAL had a spiritual power
Pure and bland like toilet soap
He could stay good by the hour
Where lesser men just couldn't cope,
Strength and Virtue's young white hope:
The lad would do good some day.

Parsifal was a tender weed
Growing tame by the banks of the Rhine.
Never could he slimly go to seed,
Never for a woman would he rise and shine.
Everyone took it for a positive sign:
The lad would do good some day.

Parsifal upped and goosed a goose,
Knocked it off and out of the sky,
Left it for dead and then turned loose
To ride in reply to a witch's cry.
She taught him by rote and smiled a sigh:
The lad would do good some day.

II. That Sir Lancelot !

The knights
Of the Round Table wore tights,
Were as able in fights
As Gable.
With lance
Held at the ready their stance
And their Teddy-Boy pants
Were steady.

Till Lance-
elot would dance
A lot a-
bout the walls of Cam-
elot.
Whenever Guinevere
Would endeavour to sneer
He'd do a pirouette
Around her oubliette
And invert himself in the crêpe suzette.
Yet !

The knights
Of the Round Table were sights,
Indulging in strangest delights:
Cavorting, disporting, in inordinate rorting.
All for the love of,
All for Lance-
Lance-
Lance-
lot.
The lot !

III. Siegfried – Heap Big

for Johnnymack

When SIEGFRIED went to hunt the boar
(Drunk as a lord and roaring for more)
Holy cap and magic sword,
Shining helmet, silver cord,
Lent their blessing to the conquering Lord !
Warrior-Hero, Archetype IV.

When Siegfried marched back from the chase
(Glory and sunshine in his face)
The tribe went wild
About Golden Child,
By evil and crassness undefiled,
Ten-Foot Whopper of the Master Race.

He was goalie for The Holy Graal,
Lone pine rider of the Rhineland trail;
Answer to all valkyries' prayers
(He had them playing musical chairs)
The tip-top, ultimate summit in squares –
But modern man has lost his tail.

IV. Son of Sir Galahad

I have never touched another
By poke or prod or shove;
But, as Every Man's My Brother,
I suppose I am in love.

With enginedrivers, farmers,
Swamis, yogis, lamas,
(Some of them under age):
And I Hate All Evil Sinners,
On beds, in bars, at dinners
In my holy rage.

I suppose I love and hate, then;
But, though my skull is thick
My Strength Is As The Strength of Ten.
Because I am a lunatic.

Bad Lad Ballad

Here is a song of two kinds of love
Enough for all, so take your pick
On the curve of the hill where the grass is fine
Or the deep of the wood where the ferns are thick.

My love had honey to soothe my thirst
Our love was strong as a windlass chain
Her hair was black as the deepest well
Her fainting tears as soft as rain.

Sing a lament for the deeds of men
For the poor, lost girl and the losing boy
Songs of love never end in joy
In the deep of the wood where the ferns are thick.

When I took another love
It wasn't wise to tell the first
Like a brandy man with a taste for wine
I had found two kinds of thirst.

My new love had just waked to love
And knew no love but mine.
He learnt there to join in sport
On the curve of the hill where the grass is fine.

I enjoyed them apart for a blissful while
When nights were full, and life complete
Till one day between wood and hill
My two loves chanced to meet.

Curse the day of that fateful chance
And curse all lovers' deceiving charms
My love lay where the ferns are thick

With my love in his arms.

Sing a lament for the loss of love
For my lonely state and my aching heart.
Now I must seek along my way
A wood and a hill that are far apart.

Blessing

for the widow of Dr Harris

Be giddy, be gaily beguiling
Be a dear now, and slip out of mourning
Who knows, but a new world is dawning
Mrs Harris, be widowed, and smiling.

Succumb
In the smartest of flattering hats
To cocktails in tight little flats
Sparkle, and pull out your plum.

Be sneaky, steal out of your prison
You've little to lose, less to fear
And a word in your ear dear;
Jesus is risen.

Ignore
The breakfast prescriptions
The dinnertime frictions ;
The doctor will see you no more.

Curse

for Doctor Harris

Doctor Harris your wife is returning
Doctor Harris her bosom is heaving
Doctor Harris the servants are leaving
Doctor Harris your alcohol's burning

Doctor Harris your future is looming
Doctor Harris there's glass in the butter
Doctor Harris the candles will gutter
Doctor Harris they're bent on exhuming

Doctor Harris your wife has been flirting
Doctor Harris your children are kissing
Doctor Harris the morphia's missing
Doctor Harris the cat is deserting

Doctor Harris they're gathering faggots
Doctor Harris the bushes will hide them
Doctor Harris your wife is beside them
Doctor Harris the maggots

Cogito Ergo Sit

Certain is a word I like
I'd like to get the rights of
Space is a place to put the Jews
Time, something Eliot writes of.

Talk of planets in their courses
Inexorable forces
Or a million laws of motion
Idle notions, wasted breath.

You can not bring it back for me
That existential certainty
The universe that ceased to be
At Bishop Berkeley's death.

Daylong Byways

Order and disorder
Are flaws within the Lens
To screw perception tight
And tight distort
Perfection to disorder,
Both flaws within the Lens,
Smears that cross to warp,
Filters there condensing
Order from distortion,
Within the Lens.

Outside, bright electronic traffic
Is pumped through arrowed paths
As pulses on the signal beam
That 1 transmits to 5 on time,
Transmitted from before this time
To receivers still half-hidden
In a mist of yesterday
Sending and receiving still.

The ends of days receiving still
Blank messages of origin
In dot and dash unmodified
Reassuring, positive
Of Motive Power powering Motive
Moving, powering all.
Such sober throbbing power, perhaps,
Will see us through this universe.

May see us through to Paradise,
Enervation of all energy
Suspended, stopt Nirvana.
For those after us, Transmission

Shall continue as before
From 9 to 5 through yesterdays,
Luncheons, loves, and wars,
This sober current singing.

Latterday saints

Hosanna, my dears!
Yapped the canonized lady in pins
On her holy own, praying through the phone
To invisible disciples' grins.
Latterday afternoon,
Appointments filled in the gilt arcade.
The chemistry glitter applied by day
Absorbs the evening accolade.
Under fluorescent haloes pterodactyl jaws
Clack to the sixty cycle light
So bright.

Here, my girl

Here is the door, the room and window
  Here is an amusing little lamp I made
Here is the green Morocco wireless set:
  It blends, don't you think, with the pigskin shade?
Here, if you read, are two thousand Penguins
  And here, right here, before you draw breath,
Here is the bed:
  Here we shall have our petty death.

Night is a sleepy Mexican stabbed at dawn

The morning is cold as the ringing alarm
Whose cold is as wide as the shower-room floor
The night was killed beneath a plaster palm
And the sun came out and shut the door.
Slam, behind it: they won't find it's
Me that did it, with a star and hid it
Quit stalling, you saw me, don't tell them, I pray you,
I'll pay you, much sunshine.
Say the bells of alarm clocks
Over floors of far shower-rooms.
When will you bribe me?
Ask the blackmailing towelracks.
Tomorrow, tomorrow, tomorrow, tomorrow,
I'll borrow, I'll borrow, I'll borrow, I'll borrow
With every day in debt to the last
To obliterate the shady past,
The doings beneath the plaster palm.

Pigeons on the grass, by crikey

Come and I'll show you a clever big park
All the trees are made of wood
The pool is just water but it's guaranteed pure
The dirty old men are really good.

If you get off the grass and into the trees
Like every good girl should
You'll find a memorial made of sand
(They can't see the trees for the wood).

It's terribly grand and belongs to death
It stares at itself in the flattened pool
Without any vanity, pleasure or show
(Death, like water, will always keep cool).

Down among the dead coins lucky men throw
There's only more cold and a concrete field
Inside the shrine is a dying black metal man
Who came back on his shield.

All around the railing dying black men stare
At the giant black metal man lying back
Back on his back for them, for them
Racked on their rack.

Here on the doorstep of death's sand castle,
Here at the gate of the House of the Dead,
We can resting, defiling, defy
With this pigeon who ratchets up, hinging head.

Weather Report

[For Jenny]

Birds like aeroplanes stultify
Those stupefying pigeon rows
Where beneath the mending shows
Going up like gentle fireworks
To heaven, as the Christian Good
Abide with him who mapped out Hell
Wrote "Here be lions", was mauled and fell
To earth in Palestine.

Cyclones screw up tight and creak
Dovetailed fretwork doves appear
Bargain swindles, far too dear
Like aeroplanes and half-dead christs:
The only show that's worth the tax
Is watching seedlings grow perhaps
And fair maidens, all in a row
Before the flight, the lions and falling.

She'll know those
Old wagon wheels
Deep in the hide of her
Wheels like doves
Flying psalms
Sing inside of her
Peel like skins
Of mandarins
Dive bomb down
Hands in gown
Love at last
Beyond the least
Of little love away

Little love away.

Think on this, perhaps of value
Could ask any trouble spent
For her, the bleating damned who went
The way of all fish and fowl and good red flesh;
Bad red herrings dragged across
Weep like others' stars
Irrelevant as motor cars
Falling over Palestine.
She'll know havens trite as pastures green
Joy like the boys grown up in summers slim
And all his boys surprise about him
Regret like a dying homosexual;
But pain is all you can not have
Home is where she stays a while
And half a drowned old lady's smile
Is all she can not give away.

These days to be are on a graph somewhere
To tear off, sunder as they're used
Losing pretends to be refused
And comes on time to the tradesman's door
Not to a nation of lost golf balls
But a golf ball lost, by who
Knowing they lose is for the few
And you can not know what hill behind.

Some of these days
She's losing losing
Love all only
Won the toss
One of these days
Some well-known product
Will be no more

The name is lost.
Faces even, now or heaven
Will be to her but other days
Sad as past is, would you tell her
She's on the losing side.

Screw up some aeroplanes and kill some gods
Bless her for a marked-down lamb
Stop her ears with honey for the ram
Where the cyclones curdle the hives;
Rush in with the air, some oxygen
Makes a good depression cure
High to low is falling sure
Love at least a lost away.

Pussy's very fond of cream

The cat is reviewing the human race
Will be fair and kind,
Fairly kindly inclined,
Will merely shrug
And wash her face.

The cat sat
On the mat, squat
On the steps in Flemish light
Will sit flat
As a black hat, hot
In the day's yellow, living night.

Her rut as hot as touch alive
Denies that needle ice
Sings in her eyes as green as sight;
High through the day's yellow
And the twilight land of the velvet mice
Rears the reminding, coming night.

She knows and sees us even now,
Sees evenly through the cold green tears
But ladylike will wait ten thousand thousand years
To shrug.

Love Play

[For Jenny]

What'll the battle be, settle the weather bee
Fingerstall fighting the recognised fee
Rumble composedly o'er the lea
Fettle fertility complacently.

Round the wattle bewitch to where
Tender the meddle man's fairy fair
Hurtle the girdle with flaxen hair
Downy down town-going any-new-where.

Render the bat with the peach-fed wing
Muscle the blunder buss sorry go ring
Pity the poor sailors having their fling
Silly down derricking shot from a sling.

Ever glide giddily through the fen
Under the bridge with the water the men
Strangle in rainbow the plastic hen
Do-si-do drowsy so, every-go-when
Do-si-do drowsy so, every-go-when.

When You Walked

When you walked just then
I saw comets flash their fire
Sky on edge
Burning men

Hell, you must have seen
All the flashing lights and fires
Up for sale
Evergreen

See from your walking how
Such sweet scissors flash, and light
Warning flares
Look out, now.

Evening Below

Evening below
Do you like it now?
Gravely know
Overcoats go.

People below
Do you care, at all?
Pavement washed
And policemen slow.

Strangers around
Do you like it yet?
Lamp posts lose
Nothing below.

So overcoats hunch
Over the slow street
Retreating below
Do you like it now?

I Don't Care

I don't care that it rains and freezes
I am safe with my strange diseases
Safer than a row of houses
Stranger than the smell of flowers is.

I don't care that I'm small and dying
Or that my off-colour nose is
Smelling through hell the pallor of roses
Now I know their god is lying.

I don't care that I'm earnest, rowing
Negligent to the cataract;
Sweet dawn comes up like an artifact
And listen, hear the phoenix crowing.

Labrador

Labradors retrievers are
Labradors retrieve
In their mouth receive
Rubber ducks, and dominoes
Shuttlecock and rabbit fur
Slipper-tongue and jacket sleeve.

Labradors appeal to all
The determined air they wear
The pride, the stride, the savoir faire,
Far from the Douglas firs they love
And the feathery caramel haunches of
The labradoresses there.

I am away to Labrador
Where the dogs, and life, are grand.
Heeling and harness are good for you.
To follow the guns in the morning dew,
The game and the prize are for the few
In Newfoundland.

If I should suffer some mishap
Come down in an alien sea
In a jumbo jet at cocktail time
I'd be in my element, free
Free to be retrieving still
Till the floes close over me.

Now that I have dared

Now that I have dared to speak
Not trusting myself, wanting to make it easy
For you to leave if you wished it
What shall I say? And how?
I shall be cheerful, yes, not grieve
That the love that we once shared
Is all mine now.

Provincial Report

From Pilate, to Caesar :- If it please Your
Omnipotent Godhead
There's an impenitent hothead
Questioning You. The native king
Won't do anything but pass the buck
Just like a Jew.

Here I am in the East with a legion or two
In a palace of pink mud among the subject Hebrew.
An oriental people, luxurious and cruel
With customs such as I and You
Wouldn't know the half of: punishments for minor crime
Barbaric and behind the times
As the Tarquin never knew.

Through our desert house the wind blows in and out
Sand is swept from the hallways hourly.
Native women entertain with primitive dancing
And in reward demand their lovers' heads.
At night we turn in our alien beds
With the heat, and the hopeless chanting.

The religious lead sad parades of heavy veiled ladies
Children from the age of three are trained to weep
The tears of mourners are all there is to lay the dust
And only the dead get any sleep.

My maniple, warmed by ancient winds
Hangs unused on my soiled sleeve
Useless to cool or clean a distressed brow
The weariest of foreheads.

Yet no one remembers a Roman governor

But for what he omits to do.
Begging Your pardon, by Your leave
What do I do with this Jew?

The Park Ward Rolls Royce

When cars are parked on a sloping road you can see underneath
Like girls on a windy day, so
Two of us thought to crawl beneath,
Dive flat on our backs to rustle about,
Squat beetles hypnotized
By chassis members, tubes of beauty
Round and hard yet warm from running.
The car was full with recent motion
Like a woman lying spent and lovely
While you make the coffee.

There we lay in the undergloom
To trace transmission, the line of power
Through the frame, through arteries. All this
Park Ward had fleshed with grace and metal,
Banner high and splayed wide, the last
Trumpeting show of the Opulent Era.

At the owner's step we surfaced, chatted
Profanely of what we'd seen, at heart
Still down there in the shadow.
Then the car revived to stride away,
Over the hill to the forbidden country,
Leaving us a pain like cold,
Or a woman, when she leaves you.

The Man Who Killed the Harbour Bridge

Was hanged at dawn last night
With streetlamps for a jury —
Lead, kindly light.

The man who shot the harbour bridge
Was stabbed to death in his room
With his mirror, the accomplice, —
Amid th'encircling gloom.

The man who killed the harbour bridge
Did it only in intention,
And lived to enjoy a quiet old age
On his Public Service pension.

Mary, call the cattle home

Oh Mary call the cattle home across the sand of Dee
Polish their horns with junipers
Measure them with callipers
And hurry on home for your tea

Oh Mary call the cattle home across the sands of Dee
On the way there's a shrine you'll find
Built to St Gorboduc, neatly designed
Genuflect three times three

Oh Mary call the cattle home across the sands of Dee
Where there's a will, I think there's a way
That, so I am told, is what people say –
It's not very far from the sea.

The United Kingdom of Great Britain and Northern Ireland

Factors and middlemen in the Strand
Sent their children out in chains
To Hawkesbury and Emu Plains
From that green, unpleasant land

In wood and peril, as pilgrims go
Unsupplied with the juice of limes
Living with scurvy and the Sunday Times
On hire from Barclays, D. C. O.

Beefeaters with free teeth now dance
For florins for their warm pale ales
For emigrants from New South Wales
Inspecting their inheritance:

Bells through fog, and the light is vague;
The days are dead and gone.
Night will follow on
Cabbages, history and plague.

Autobus, My Autobus

Beasts who daily ease their gears
By hill and curve in suburban journeys
Lie at depot greenly dumb.

Under neons the patient rears
Washed and waiting, alike as peas
Abide the fifty cycle hum.

4 a. m. Faces blue at the jaws
With sandwiches for a thousand miles
And driving feet still bedroom-numb

Horde toward the unwary, devoted doors,
Leadenly on down diesel aisles
The black conductors come.

I Used To Like

I used to love young Jesus Christ
And all his family
His ministering angels and enemies of course,
But
Remorse, remorse, remorse, remorse
Was all they gave to me.

When Adam delved

When Adam delved
For unseemly roots
Who overseered
And ate the fruits?

When Eve span
Her web of lies
Who sprang the trap
And spoiled the prize?

O for a God to befriend us
With fruits to send us
A Devil to tempt us
A worm to end us!

"Sometimes" said Adam
"For variety's sake
I go to the loneliness
By the lake."

"I too," said Eve
"Even that we share —
Finish your digging
I'll meet you there."

"Damn" said Adam
"Is Adam allowed
No lake to himself?
Two's a crowd."

Two knew loneliness
By the lake:
He called it, God;
Eve called it Snake.

With you here beside me

With you here beside me
Everything is fine
I can peek, and prove
Your eyes are watching mine

But can you stay forever
Giving years the lie
Till my eyes are daisies
And my blood is dry

Surely you can notice
All the extra years
Looking back, unblinking
Right behind my ears.

I haven't long before you
Lift your eyes, and know
Others' eyes for watching
Other's lines to toe

A hit parade of stand-ins
Wants my job tonight
Collars wide for love
Heads afloat and heels alight

Hang on tight tonight, now
Watching years go by
Till my eyes are diamonds
And my love is dry.

Three, the Rivals

I
Beginnings are fine
And finely pinned
As the evening's intent
Leans to the wind.

The lady who dines
In the Humber Hawk
And draws you inside
Where the quiet talk

Takes a glass of quinine
At a quarter of nine
If you and who else
Will brighten the scene.

The gentleman smiles
In the certain way
That invites you to cruise
About the bay.

Lift all anchor
The gentleman frowns
Smiling with money
Handyman drowns.

II
Abandoning
Children here, ladies of cars
Deny all care to sly compliers
Crazed aged urns presume with the stars
Other shy desires.

Carpentered
Park, bazaar of uncertain joys
Lamp-marooned in pools of grasses
Where lilymen smile at the lampshade boys
Their wilder graces.

Recovering
Hour by hour, this night dissolved
In a pool of remembrance, ceases
To long for rest in lovings resolved
By the plane trees.

III
Bodies in heat
And souls in season
The kill is the hunter's
Excuse for a reason

With Handyman milked
By the wandering herds
Bread cast on the waters
Is for the birds

With the corpses of evening
Left for the jackal gnome
Any minute the sheltering
Cows come home.

At St Stephen's

Hullo, yellow-haired feller

Saunter in, hunker down
Unwrap your King Street takeaway
Squeeze your eyes against the sky.

You started off a block away
Undesired, so masterless.
The Falcon they conceived you in
Rusts in Federation Lane.

Dogs invest a tree that shades
The stones of a settling nobleman
Whose motto mocks, "While I live I hope"
In a tongue unspoken.

The crow they started dives on you
As the trammeling Eagle
To cup the cheek of Ganymede
Flew over seas.

They hunt you up and out
Flushed to the street, to what
You don't yet know.

Yellow-haired feller, Hullo.

Flora Shares A Prayer

(by Katherine's dog Flora, when Katherine Cummings was in hospital recovering from heart bypass surgery)

Gone off to change again, she can't resist a change
She'll be back, back soon, soon now
Though sage deep-puddled eyes will vow
To heal distemper, cure her mange.

I can't protect her there where
She sojourns among unvisited trees.
But to rid her of that sepulchral wheeze
Is any self-respecting bitch's prayer.

I pray to see her pumping, jumping, barking with glee
Over the blossom that yelps on the bough.
May her love live on in the heart of a cow
To kick up her heels, come gambol with me.

Gull in Waterloo

From the Southern Sung
A vase for twigs, for a stalk in bud
Whiter than a dove
Less dense than the sky

Flickered at our window
The faded froth of the shore
Made moonlight in the sun
Clear down to the ground

Where the Koori touch, and play
Between blue oblong streets
Her feathers spread to show
Pale shadows glance below.

Beyond the light of day
She left to retread the surf
Left on the matchbox patch of turf
No clarity of grey.

From the Southern Sung

Land Fall

Doors opened on the scent of light and tea
That we stole past in cold and fear unseen.
A direct hit where our life had been;
Ahead the peaks, then wastes, the bucketing sea.

Guides urged us through the lanes, the mines, the slope
Of sour herbs, of metal scraps, of frozen sand
To their plane that followed a river, plains, land
To the end of the earth, black water, a night in hope

Of paradise, the airport a warm, bright fair.
Sailing from the palms, the docks, the shore
For the hiccuping stars, then the splintering wave
Treading water to survive, hold up, save
For this dust, held under dead eyes, their unknown law.
Till this is over, treading the bare air.

Naughty boy went overboard

Naughty boy went overboard
Toward another boat.
Laughter fell on water from
Phosphorescence underneath
Another buoy afloat.

Such small fingers at the gunwales
Pull me up and out
Dry me down among your friends
Until envy or the bends
Turn me inside out.

Then recovered on the deck
Safe as in the years to be
Drily, warmly, comfortably
I'll slip quietly overboard
To be me.

Newtown Pip

Newtown Pip comes scootering by
Red Rattler tickets in her velvet clutch
Scootering close enough to touch
Her friends so best, with a five so high.

One darting eye in a lengthy car
Its onset dammed by a light gone red
Dreams grey tollway fungal spread
Down Connex Way to Malabar.

"Here the people throng and mill
They even know each other's names.
Let's sell them old SIM City games
We'll bring with us from Betaville."

The nightmare seems it's come to stay
Until the King Street light goes green.
The invader driven from the scene
Takes with him the dry, the grey.

It was just a fleeting dream
Dissolved in a macchiato sip.
Scootering off goes Newtown Pip
To coach her cycle polo team.

Oh, my King

Oh, my King
Point the way
Call the morning
Wake the day.

Gain the rise
Spread the sky
See the lake
Watch us fly.

From your zenith
Unfurl the air
Beyond the known
Presume, and dare.

Descend and rule
Lay down the law
Upon the slope
Along the shore.

Go now slow
Beckon the night.
Follow the course I showed you.
Get it right.

Somewhere in the Broken Heart

Somewhere in the broken heart
Somewhere sweet and poisoning
Drawn by crook and torn by hook
Blood tears start.

The last day of the frost
Choristers without a brain
Break the glass, fall back in pain
Lost, lost.

Somewhere in the broken heart
Adrift, amiss, astray
Somehow, just the other day
We fell apart.

Michael

Michael —
I keep thinking.
I live at Waterloo. Are you in town much?
I imagine that you live in the mountains. I spend a lot of time on trains, and one of them goes up mountains.
Do you drink coffee? Is there somewhere that we could meet for coffee? Chardonnay? Tea?
Do let me know.